Fish

Please visit our web site at: www.garethstevens.com
For a free color catalog describing Gareth Stevens Publishing's
list of high-quality books and multimedia programs, call
1-800-542-2595 (USA) or 1-800-387-3178 (Canada).
Gareth Stevens Publishing's fax: (414) 332-3567.

Library of Congress Cataloging-in-Publication Data

Richardson, Joy.
    Fish / Joy Richardson. — North American ed.
      p. cm. — (Variety of life)
    Includes bibliographical references and index.
    ISBN 0-8368-4503-X (lib. bdg.)
    1. Fishes—Juvenile literature. I. Title.
  QL617.2.R5289   2005
  597—dc22   2004056760

This North American edition first published in 2005 by
Gareth Stevens Publishing
A WRC Media Company
330 West Olive Street, Suite 100
Milwaukee, Wisconsin 53212 USA

This U.S. edition copyright © 2005 by Gareth Stevens, Inc.
Original editions copyright © 1993 and 2003 by Franklin Watts.
First published in 1993 by Franklin Watts, 96 Leonard Street,
London EC2A 4XD, England.

Franklin Watts Editors: Sarah Ridley and Sally Luck
Franklin Watts Designer: Janet Watson
Picture Research: Sarah Moule

Gareth Stevens Editor: Dorothy L. Gibbs
Gareth Stevens Designer: Kami Koenig

Picture credits: Bruce Coleman, Ltd. – 13, 21; Frank Lane Picture
Agency – cover, 17 (bottom); Oxford Scientific Films – 3, 7, 9, 15, 23;
Planet Earth Pictures – 11, 19, 25, 27; Science Photo Library – 17 (top).

Printed in the United States of America

1 2 3 4 5 6 7 8 9 09 08 07 06 05

Variety of Life

Joy Richardson

GARETH**STEVENS**

GS

PUBLISHING

A WRC Media Company

Contents

Words that appear in the glossary are printed in
boldface type the first time they occur in the text.

Thousands of Fish

There are more than twenty thousand different kinds of fish in the world. Some fish live in salty seas and oceans. Others live in **freshwater** rivers, lakes, and ponds.

All fish have bodies that are made for living in water. The bodies of some fish are bigger than a person. Other fish have bodies that are smaller than a fingernail.

Besides being many different sizes, fish come in many different shapes and colors.

Fish Eggs

Female fish lay eggs to **reproduce**.

Most fish lay their eggs in water. The eggs usually contain tiny bubbles of air or oil to help them float.

Some fish lay eggs that stick together or **cling** to weeds or rocks.

Most fish eggs are no bigger than the head of a pin — and other creatures like to eat them! **Cod** lay millions of eggs at a time to make sure that some will **survive**.

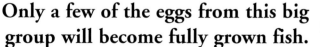

Only a few of the eggs from this big group will become fully grown fish.

From Egg to Fish

After fish lay their eggs, they usually swim away. Some fish, however, carry their eggs around with them.

A female seahorse lays her eggs in a **pouch** on the front of a male seahorse's body. The male seahorse carries the eggs in his pouch until they **hatch**.

When a baby fish hatches, it is not completely formed. A baby fish that has just hatched is called a **larva**.

A fish larva stays attached to its egg until its body grows **fins**. While it is attached to the egg, the larva feeds on the egg's **yolk**.

This male seahorse has a pouch full of eggs.

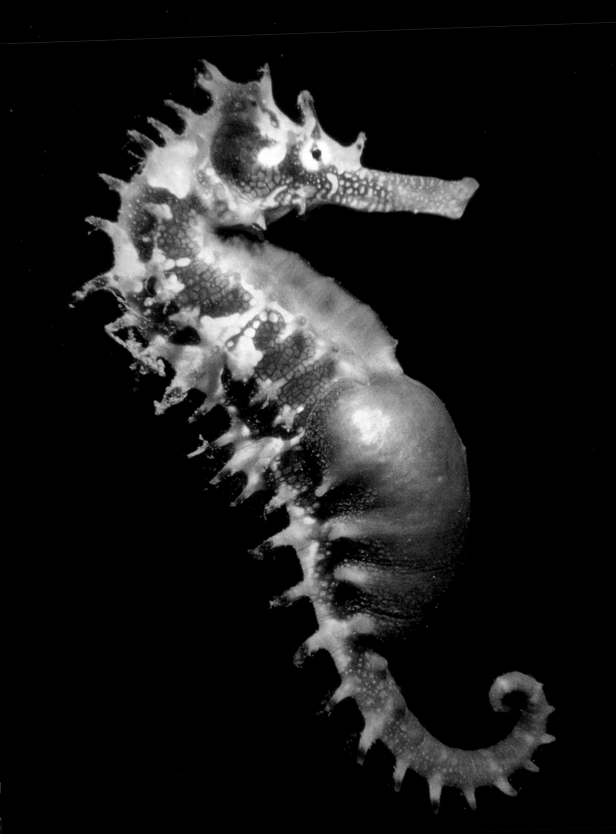

Scales

The body of a fish is covered with **scales**. Scales are little plates of tough skin. One end of each scale is attached to the fish.

The scales on a fish are arranged in **overlapping** rows. As the fish moves and bends, its scales slide over each other.

Sharks have very rough skin. Their scales are like tiny pointed teeth.

A fish has the same number of scales all its life, but as the fish gets older, each scale grows bigger. **Growth rings** on the scales show the age of the fish.

Dace are a type of freshwater fish. Although dace are small fish, they each have hundreds of tiny silver scales. ➡

Water Colors

Lots of fish are a silvery color, but fish come in many other colors, too.

The bright colors of some fish help protect them from their enemies. Sometimes, a fish's colors or **markings** even warn enemies to stay away.

Many fish are a shiny, light color underneath and a darker color on top. From below, these fish look like light flickering on the **surface** of the water. From above, they look the same color as the dark water around them.

The silvery undersides on these fish make the fish hard to see from below.

Fish Skeletons

Every fish has a **skeleton** inside it.

The skeletons of most fish are made of bones. A thick backbone runs down the middle of a fish. Long, thin bones spread outward from the backbone to support the fish's **muscles** and fins.

The skeletons of sharks and rays do not have bones. They are made of tough **gristle**, called cartilage.

An X ray of a fish (*top*) shows the fish's skeleton. An eel (*bottom*) has a long backbone that bends as this snakelike fish wiggles through the water.

Swimming

The bodies of fish are made for swimming. Fish are **streamlined**. Water flows smoothly around their pointed heads and over their **oval** bodies. A streamlined body makes swimming easy.

Fish swim by using their fins. They swish their tail fins from side to side and use their other fins to hold them **upright** and steady.

Sticklebacks use their side fins to paddle gently backward and forward. Unlike most fish, a stickleback does not have scales on its body. Its name comes from the two or three thorny spines it has along its back.

A large grouper has powerful tail fins to help it swim through the ocean.

Breathing Underwater

Like all other animals, fish need **oxygen** to stay alive. Because water contains less oxygen than air, fish have their own way of breathing.

Fish have **gills**. To breathe, a fish takes a mouthful of water, then closes its mouth and pushes the water through its gills.

The gills of a fish contain thin tubes of blood that soak up oxygen from the water. The water comes out of the fish through the gill openings on the sides of its head.

This carp is taking in a mouthful of water.

Fish Senses

Fish have the same five senses as other animals. They can see, smell, hear, taste, and feel.

Fish eyes are made to see through water. Fish have no eyelids so they never close their eyes, not even when they sleep.

Fish pick up smells from water flowing through their **nostrils**. Their ears are inside their heads, and they can taste with their chins. Some fish use **feelers** for tasting as well as for touching.

Unlike other animals, fish have a sixth sense, called a **sense line**. The sense line runs along the side of a fish and tells the fish where other objects are in the water.

This fish uses its long yellow feelers for tasting.

Fish Schools

Most young fish swim together in groups.
A group of fish is called a school.

Herring always swim together in schools.
The sense lines along their sides help keep
them in position.

Many fish make long journeys in groups.
Schools of salmon swim across the oceans,
then find their way back to their home rivers
to lay eggs.

Fishing boats go where they will find schools
of fish swimming or eating together.

**Swimming in a school helps protect fish
from attacks by larger sea creatures.**

Eating

Without arms or hands, fish have to catch their food with their mouths.

Most fish have sharp teeth inside their mouths. When old teeth fall out, new teeth grow in to replace them.

To find food, some fish use their feelers. Cod use their feelers to search for worms and **shellfish** on the **seabed**.

A shark bites and tears its food with its strong, pointed teeth.

Fish Facts

There are all different kinds of fish in the world, but they are the same in many ways.

- All fish hatch from eggs.

- All fish are made for living in water. They are all **cold-blooded** animals that breathe through gills, and they all have a backbone and fins.

- The bodies of most fish are covered with scales.

Jellyfish and starfish are not really fish. Their bodies do not work the same way the bodies of real fish do.

For More Facts . . .

Books

Fish. What's the Difference (series).
  Stephen Savage (Raintree)

Hello Fish! Visiting the Coral Reef. Sylvia A. Earle
  (National Geographic)

Hungry, Hungry Sharks! Joanna Cole (Random House)

What Is a Fish? The Science of Living Things (series).
  Bobbie D. Kalman (Crabtree)

Web Sites

Cool Kids' Fishin'
  www.ncfisheries.net/kids/

New World Publication's Marine Life Learning Center:
  Kid's Corner
  www.fishid.com/facts.htm

Yahooligans Ask Earl: Fish
  yahooligans.yahoo.com/content/ask_earl/category?c=68

Glossary

cling: to hold onto tightly

cod: a commonly eaten fish found mainly in cold waters

cold-blooded: having a body temperature that gets warmer or cooler with the temperature of its surroundings

feelers: long, thin body parts, usually sticking out from the head, that are used for feeling and, sometimes, tasting

fins: the movable body parts on the back, sides, and tail of a fish that help the fish swim, steer, and balance in water

freshwater: describing bodies of water that are not salty

gills: the body parts that make fish able to breathe in water

gristle: the tough, musclelike tissue found in certain meats

growth rings: markings that show the number of growth periods an animal or plant has lived through, with one ring for each growth period

hatch: to break out of an egg

larva: the first form of most animals that come from eggs

markings: marks, especially particular shapes or patterns

muscles: the strong, stretchy tissues that make bones and other body parts able to move

nostrils: the openings, or holes, on the outside of a nose, through which air enters for breathing and smelling

oval: egg-shaped

overlapping: one on top of another but covering only part of the layer underneath

oxygen: a colorless, odorless, tasteless gas that all animals need to breathe to stay alive

pouch: a kind of pocket on an animal's body, formed by loose or stretchy skin

reproduce: to have babies

scales: thin, hard flakes that cover and protect a fish's body

seabed: the ocean floor

sense line: a line of nerve endings, along the side of a fish's body, that sense changes in the movement of the water

shellfish: water animals, such as crabs and clams, that have hard coverings, or shells, on the outsides of their bodies

skeleton: a shape made of bones that forms the body of an animal

streamlined: having a shape that allows air and water to flow easily around it

surface: the top or outside layer of something

survive: stay alive

upright: straight up, or vertical; rightside up

yolk: the part of an egg that provides food for the animal growing inside the egg

Index